Covered Calls for Working People

Earn Weekly Income with Options

by Adrian Gregory

DISCLAIMER: This book is for educational purposes only. I am not a licensed financial advisor, broker, or planner. The strategies described are based on personal experience and are not guarantees of results. Trading options involves risk, including potential loss of principal.

Readers should do their own research or consult a licensed professional before making any financial decisions.

ISBN: 979-8-9938323-0-2

Published by Adrian Gregory

Castalian Springs, Tennessee

For Megan, Ellie, and Everly—thank you for believing in me. All that I do, I do for you. As the Lord has called me to be a husband and father, and I could not be more blessed to call you my family. I love you.

Table of Contents

Preface

I wrote this book because I wanted to share a simple, repeatable way to grow income that anyone with a small brokerage account can use.

When I first started learning about options, I was overwhelmed. Wall Street professionals made it sound complicated on purpose, I believe. It was more of a gamble than anything, but when I figured out covered calls, everything clicked: steady, weekly income with limited risk.

This book isn't theory—it's real-world experience, explained in plain English. My goal is to make sure the average working person can understand and apply this strategy, without needing a finance degree.

— Adrian Gregory

Chapter 1: Why You're Here

Most working people feel stuck. You work hard, you try to save, and you do your best to invest responsibly. But let's be honest — the system doesn't make it easy:

- Banks pay you pennies in interest. While they make trillions off of your money.

- The stock market feels like a gamble. You might win, or lose it all!

- Side hustles take too much time when you're already stretched thin. If you're like me and working 14 hours a day most days, and the money still doesn't grow the way you want it too. You need passive income. You need your money to make money.

It's no wonder most people give up on the idea of building real wealth.

But what if I told you there's a way to take the stocks you already own and use them to **generate steady cash flow, week after week**? What if your brokerage account could act like a paycheck machine, producing small, reliable amounts of income — the kind that add up over time?

That's what covered calls can do.

The "Lightbulb" Moment

When I first discovered covered calls, it felt like someone finally handed me a set of keys Wall Street had been hiding. I researched looking for the part I must have been missing, because I didn't think it could be that easy. I didn't need to be a millionaire. I didn't need a finance degree. I just needed:

- A brokerage account that allowed options.

- 100 shares of stock.

- The willingness to learn a straightforward strategy.

That's it. No gambling. No chasing lottery tickets. Just a method to earn extra money from something I already owned.

(*My First Covered Call: I still remember the first time I clicked "sell" on a covered call. It wasn't for a big payout — in fact, it was only five dollars. I owned 100 shares of* **MVIS (MicroVision)** *and decided to sell a $1.50 strike call option expiring the following week.*

- *Strike price: $1.50*

- *Premium collected: $5.00*

- *Expiration: August 8*

When the order filled, I saw the confirmation: "1 contract at $0.05 filled, credit $4.96 after fees. [pictured below]

It might not sound like much, but it was a turning point for me. That $5 wasn't a gift, it wasn't luck, and it wasn't overtime wages — it was money I created by putting my shares to work.

I realized that if I could do this once, I could do it again and again. And if $5 was possible on a small trade, what if I had 500 shares to sell, that is $25 a week.

*That small trade gave me the confidence to keep learning. It wasn't about the amount — it was about **proving the strategy worked** in my own hands.)*

Sell MVIS $1.5 Call 8/8		$5.00
Individual · Jul 31		1 contract at $0.05
Type	**Position effect**	**Time in force**
Limit Sell	Open	Good for day
Submitted	**Quantity**	**Account**
7/31, 11:12 AM CDT	1	Individual
Status	**Filled quantity**	**Filled**
Filled	1 contract at $0.05	7/31, 11:12 AM CDT
Limit price	**Est credit**	**Est regulatory fees**
$0.05	$4.96	$0.04

Who This Book Is For

This book isn't for hedge fund managers or full-time traders. It's for:

- The dad with a small retirement account who wants to squeeze out extra cash.

- The mom building a portfolio for her family's future.

- The young worker tired of watching their savings just sit there doing nothing.

- Anyone who wants a **realistic, practical side income** without needing to gamble.

If that's you, you're in the right place.

What This Book Will Give You

In the chapters ahead, I'm going to:

1. Break down **what a covered call is** (in plain English).

2. Show you exactly **how to sell one** step by step.

3. Share **real-world examples** with actual numbers.

4. Warn you about the **risks and mistakes** people make.

5. Give you a blueprint to **turn this into weekly income**.

You'll be able to walk away from this book not just understanding covered calls, but ready to place your first trade.

The Big Picture

Here's the truth: you won't get rich overnight. Covered calls aren't a lottery ticket. But they are one of the simplest, safest ways for regular people to turn stocks into **steady income**.

Think of it like this:

- Owning stock is like owning a house.

- Selling a covered call is like renting out a spare room.

- You keep the house, but you also get paid on the side.

That's what covered calls are: a way to make your stocks pay you rent, week after week.

Chapter 2:
What is a Covered Call?

When people first hear the word *options,* they usually think "complicated," "risky," or "that's for Wall Street only." But a covered call is probably the most beginner-friendly option strategy out there. If you can understand renting out a house, you can understand a covered call.

The Rental Property Analogy

Imagine you own a house. You can live in it, of course. But you can also rent it out and collect rent every month.

Now, imagine instead of a house, you own 100 shares of a stock. A covered call is simply a way of "renting out" those shares. You don't give them away, you don't lose them, but someone pays you money (called a *premium*) for the right to buy them from you at a certain price at a set time. The "contract" gives the buyer a right to buy 100 shares of stock at the set price (strike price) before or on the expiration date of the contract.

That's it. Simple, right?

Breaking It Down

A covered call has three key parts:

1. **The Stock You Own** – This is your "house." You must already own at least 100 shares to sell one call contract. That is the tough part you may think, but there are affordable stocks with option availability.

2. **The Strike Price** – This is the price at which you agree to sell your shares if the buyer decides to exercise the option. Think of it as "the deal price." It is the price you think best, and should

always be a price higher than the price you bought the stock at, your "average price paid." (Example: your average price paid is $9.71, and you sell a contract with a strike price of $10.00 with an expiration date of the following Friday. The premium (ask/bid price) is .10 cents per share. You sell the contract and get the .10 per share [$10] right then.)

3. **The Expiration Date** – This is how long the deal lasts. Most covered calls are sold for one week or one month at a time. Some are quarterly. At market close on the expiration date, if the stock is not above the strike price, you keep the premium and the contract expires worthless.

When you sell the call, the buyer pays you **cash up front** — that's the premium. Whether the buyer ever uses the option or not, you keep that premium. THAT IS THE INCOME!

What Can Happen?

There are only three possible outcomes when you sell a covered call:

1. **Stock Stays the Same or Drops**

   o The buyer doesn't want to purchase your shares.

   o You keep your stock *and* the premium.

   o Example: You sell a $10 call, stock stays at $9 → you keep it all.

2. **Stock Goes Up a Little (But Stays Below the Strike Price)**

   o Same outcome: you keep the stock and the premium.

   o Example: You sell a $10 call, stock rises from $9.50 to $9.90 → you win.

3. **Stock Goes Above the Strike Price**

   o You keep the premium, but you have to sell your shares at the strike price.

- Example: You sell a $10 call, stock jumps to $11 → you sell at $10, still making profit, but you "miss out" on gains above $10.

Notice: in every case, you get to keep the premium. That's why this strategy can feel like collecting rent. You keep the money for the sold contract either way, and even if the shares are "called away", you still get the money back for the shares including the profit up to the strike price. So, your stock you bought at an average price of $9.71 was at $10.15 at market close on the expiration date. The strike price was for $10. Your shares are called away. You keep the $10 for the premium, you get the $9.71 back per share, PLUS the .29 cent per share ($29) profit. You only missed out on the .15 cent ($15) profit that was possible if you sold the stock yourself. If it would have expired worthless, you would just sell another contract at a new strike price and expiration and collect the premium. Again and again and again!

Why It's "Covered"

You're called "covered" because you already own the stock. This makes it safe compared to "naked calls," where you're selling contracts without having the shares to back it up (that's where people can get into serious trouble).

With covered calls, the worst-case scenario is:

- Your stock goes down (you'd lose anyway, but at least you collected premium to soften the blow).
- Or your stock goes way up (you sell it for less profit than you could have made, but you still walk away with cash in hand).

A Quick Example

Let's say you own 100 shares of XYZ stock at $20 each.

- You sell a covered call with a $22 strike price expiring in 1 week.

- The buyer pays you $50 up front (the premium).

Now:

- If the stock stays under $22 → you keep your shares + $50.

- If the stock goes above $22 → you sell at $22, making $200 profit on the shares + $50 premium.

- If the stock drops to $19 → your shares lose $100 in value, but the $50 premium cushions the loss.

The Lightbulb Moment

Here's what makes covered calls exciting: **you're turning a static investment into an income machine.** Instead of just waiting for a stock to "someday" go up, you get paid every week (or month) for owning it. (There is also a way to make money selling contracts with agreement to buy a stock at a certain price. This is called a "Put option, and should only be done if you want 100 shares of the stock, and want to get in at that price you sold the contract at. We'll get into that later.)

Chapter 3: Getting Set Up

Before you can sell your first covered call, you need the right tools. The good news? You probably already have most of them. Setting up to trade covered calls doesn't require Wall Street connections or complicated platforms. All you need is a brokerage account, approval to trade options, and at least 100 shares of a stock.

Step 1: Choosing a Brokerage

Not all brokerages are created equal. Some make options trading simple and accessible, while others bury it under layers of confusing menus. The main thing to look for is whether the broker supports **options trading** and gives you a clean interface. I personally use Robinhood, but it is what I am used to as well.

Here are a few popular choices:

- **Robinhood** – Simple interface, easy for beginners, commission-free.

- **Webull** – Free as well, with more detailed charts and data.

- **Fidelity** – Great for long-term investors who also want to sell covered calls.

- **TD Ameritrade / Schwab** – Professional-grade tools, but a steeper learning curve.

(I used to trade on Public trading app. Really great, and only moved to Robinhood because they offered joint accounts which I wanted with my wife. Both have options and are simple interfaces.)

Step 2: Getting Options Approval

When you open a brokerage account, you'll usually only have permission to buy and sell stocks. To trade options, you need to request **options trading approval.**

- This is a short questionnaire where the broker asks about your investing experience and income.

- Don't panic — for covered calls, you only need **Level 1 or Level 2** approval (the lowest tier). This is usually granted automatically.

- Once approved, the "Options" tab will appear for every stock you own. Instead of clicking "buy" or "sell", you pick "trade options."

Step 3: Owning 100 Shares

Here's the rule: **1 option contract = 100 shares.**

That means you need to own at least 100 shares of a stock to sell one covered call. If you own 200 shares, you can sell two contracts.

TIP: You don't need to start with expensive stocks like Apple or Tesla. If those are out of reach, consider:

- **Dividend stocks** under $10/share (like AGNC) They pay 14-15% dividend yield (annual yield paid out monthly) you would get to make the money from the premiums as well as the dividend unless the shares are called away prior to ex dividend date.)

- **ETFs** like QYLD or SPY, which allow covered calls and are more diversified.

- **Mid-priced stocks** where you can afford 100 shares without tying up your whole account.

(My personal one at the moment is Opendoor (OPEN). It is volatile, so the price swings are higher, but the premiums offered are higher due to that. They offer weekly options that expire Friday at market close. At the time of writing this the price for OPEN is $4.40 per share. So $440 dollars will get you 100 shares.)

Step 4: Picking the Right Stock

Not every stock makes sense for covered calls. You want something **stable enough** that it doesn't collapse overnight, but also **active enough** to generate decent premiums.

Good covered call candidates:

- Stocks you're happy to hold long-term (even if they don't move much).

- Dividend stocks (so you earn income two ways: dividends + premiums).

- ETFs (built-in diversification, usually safer).

Avoid:

- Penny stocks because they are too volatile. (I do use OPEN which is volatile, but I don't mind if the shares are called away. I will just buy them back when the price goes down, or sell a Put option contract at the price I want to get in at.)

- Extremely high-growth stocks (you risk missing big moves, but you can always sell contracts with higher strike prices, but the premiums will be lower. Pick a price the stock is in your opinion least likely to reach by expiration date. Watch out around earnings calls, as stocks usually do wild swings around that time).

Step 5: Funding Your Account

You'll need to deposit enough cash to buy 100 shares of your chosen stock. For example:

- 100 shares of a $10 stock = $1,000.

- 100 shares of a $25 stock = $2,500.

- 100 shares of a $100 stock = $10,000.

This is your "base." Once you own those shares, you can begin selling covered calls against them week after week. You may think that is too much money, but the moment you sell the covered call you get some of that money back.

Step 6: Get Comfortable with the Options Chain

Every broker has something called an **options chain**. This is just a list of all available call and put contracts for a stock, organized by strike price and expiration date.

It looks confusing at first, but here's all you need to focus on for covered calls:

- The **strike price** (at what price you agree to sell your stock).

- The **expiration date** (when the contract ends).

- The **premium** (how much you get paid).

That's it. Don't let all the numbers intimidate you — you only need three columns.

Step 7: Mindset Check

Before you hit "sell" on your first call, it helps to set expectations:

- Covered calls are about **steady cash flow**, not hitting home runs.

- Think in terms of **weeks and months**, not single trades.

- Focus on learning the process, not chasing the biggest payouts.

At this point, you'll be fully equipped: a broker, 100 shares, and options approval. In the next chapter, we'll walk step by step through actually placing your first covered call.

Chapter 4: Step-by-Step Guide to Selling a Covered Call

You've got your brokerage account set up, you've been approved for options trading, and you own at least 100 shares of stock. Now it's time to actually sell your first covered call.

Don't worry—the process is simpler than it looks. Once you've done it once, it will feel as easy as buying or selling a regular stock.

Step 1: Choose Your Stock

Pick one of the stocks you already own at least 100 shares of. For this example, let's say you have **100 shares of AGNC at $9.70**.

Step 2: Open the Options Chain

- In your brokerage app, go to your stock's page.
- Tap on **"Trade Options"** or **"Options"** (the wording varies by broker).
- You'll see a list of contracts, sorted by expiration dates. This is the **options chain**. Don't let it intimidate you.

Step 3: Select an Expiration Date

Each row you see in the chain is tied to an **expiration date** — the day the contract ends.

- **Weekly options**: Expire every Friday (great for faster income).
- **Monthly options**: Expire the third Friday of each month (more stable, less management).

Beginners often start with **weekly expirations** because they get faster feedback and income. For this example, let's choose next Friday's date.

Step 4: Pick a Strike Price

Now you'll see a list of strike prices (the price at which you'd agree to sell your shares).

- If you want more premium, you pick a strike closer to the current stock price.
- If you want less risk of being "called away," you pick a higher strike price.

Example:

- Stock price = $9.70
- Strike price chosen = $10.00

This means: if the stock rises above $10 by expiration, you'll sell your shares at $10.

Step 5: Look at the Premium

Next to each strike price, you'll see a **premium value** (often shown as $0.05, $0.10, $0.20, etc.). Multiply this number by 100 (since 1 contract = 100 shares).

Example:

- Premium = $0.20
- Contract size = 100
- **Total premium = $20**

This $20 goes straight into your account the moment you sell the contract.

Strike price	Chance of profit	Volume	% Change	Change	Price
$13	98.44%	0	0.00%	$0.00	$0.01 +
$12	97.83%	0	0.00%	$0.00	$0.01 +
$11	90.47%	65	0.00%	$0.00	$0.05 +
$10	69.77%	529	+9.52%	+$0.02	$0.23 +

Step 6: Place the Order

- Choose **"Sell to Open"** (very important — you're selling the option, not buying it).
- Enter the number of contracts (1 contract = 100 shares).
- Set the **limit price** (the premium you're willing to accept).
- Review the trade.
- Hit **Submit**.

Your broker will then either fill the order instantly or wait until someone buys your contract at your chosen price.

Step 7: What Happens Next?

Now you sit back and wait until expiration day.

Here's what can happen:

1. **Stock stays below $10** → You keep your shares and the $20 premium.

2. **Stock goes above $10** → You sell your shares at $10, and still keep the $20 premium.

3. **Stock falls hard** → You keep your shares (which are worth less), but the $20 premium cushions the loss a bit.

In every case, you keep the premium.

Step 8: Rinse and Repeat

The beauty of covered calls is consistency. The moment one contract expires, you can sell another one for the following week. Each time, you collect another premium. Over months and years, this creates steady cash flow that compounds over time.

Example Trade Recap

Let's revisit the **AGNC $10 call example**:

- Shares owned: 100 at $9.70 = $970
- Sold covered call: $10 strike, 1 week out
- Premium: $20

Outcomes:

- Stock stays at $9.70 → Keep $20 + shares
- Stock rises to $10.50 → Sell at $10, keep $30 profit on shares + $20 premium = $50 gain

- Stock falls to $9.20 → Lose $50 on shares, but offset by $20 premium = $30 net loss (smaller than if you hadn't sold the call, and you still have the shares which typically rebound over time.)

And that's it — you've just placed your first covered call. Once you've done it once or twice, it becomes second nature.

Chapter 5: Real-World Examples

Now that you understand the mechanics of a covered call, let's look at what it feels like in practice. Real numbers, real trades — and yes, real money.

Covered calls don't have to be big. In fact, my very first one was tiny. But that first trade was the turning point: it proved the strategy works, even at the smallest scale.

My First Covered Call: MVIS

I remember placing my first covered call on **MVIS (MicroVision)**. It wasn't a huge stock. I didn't make hundreds of dollars. But it taught me more than all the articles I had read.

Here's what happened:

- Stock: MVIS
- Shares owned: 100
- Strike price: $1.50
- Expiration: 8/8
- Premium: $5.00

The order filled immediately: *1 contract at $0.05, credit $4.96 after fees.*

It may not sound like much, but that $5 was money I didn't have the day before. And I didn't have to do anything except own the shares and place the order. That's it!

What did I learn?

- The process was simple.
- The premium showed up instantly in my account.
- Even with a small trade, the system worked.

That first $5 proved to me that I could repeat the process with larger, more consistent stocks and build a real income stream.

Dividend Stock Example: AGNC

One of my favorite covered call stocks is **AGNC**, a real estate investment trust that also pays dividends.

- Shares owned: 100 @ $9.70 ($970 total)
- Sold call: $10 strike, expiring in 1 week
- Premium collected: $20

Outcomes:

- If AGNC stays under $10 → I keep my shares + $20.
- If AGNC goes above $10 → I sell at $10, earning $30 profit on shares + $20 premium = $50 gain.
- If AGNC drops → My $20 premium softens the loss.

Bonus: AGNC pays a monthly dividend. That means I earn from **dividends + covered calls**, a double income stream. This can earn you over 50% or more on your investment if done correctly.

ETF Example: QYLD

Another strategy is using ETFs (exchange-traded funds). They're more diversified, which makes them safer for beginners.

Example trade:

- Shares owned: 100 of QYLD @ $17 ($1,700 total)
- Sold call: $18 strike, expiring in 2 weeks

- Premium collected: $30

Outcomes:

- QYLD stays under $18 → I keep shares + $30.
- QYLD goes over $18 → I sell at $18, locking in $100 gain on shares + $30 premium.
- QYLD falls → $30 premium cushions the dip.

The key here is safety: ETFs don't swing wildly like single stocks, so your income is steadier. Also, this is another great paying dividend stock. They pay over 10% APY paid out in monthly payments to its investors. Guess what the stock does? It is a COVERED CALL ETF! They take profits from covered calls and pay out to other people. If they are paying out 10-11%, how much do you think they are really making?

The Lesson From These Examples

Whether it's $5, $20, or $30, the process is the same. The premium arrives instantly, and it's yours to keep no matter what.

- Small trade (MVIS): Gave me confidence.
- Dividend stock (AGNC): Gave me double income.
- ETF (QYLD): Gave me stability.
- Opendoor (OPEN) gave me higher premiums.

Covered calls scale with your account. If you can make $5, you can make $50. If you can make $50, you can make $500. The math multiplies — the system doesn't change. As they say, it takes money to make money. So the more you reinvest those premiums to accumulate 100 more shares of a stock, that is one more contract you can sell.

Chapter 6: Risks and Downsides

Covered calls are one of the safest option strategies out there, but nothing in investing is risk-free. To be successful long term, you need to understand both the strengths *and* the limitations of this strategy.

1. The Stock Can Drop Hard

The biggest risk is simple: you still own the stock. If your stock falls from $20 to $15, the $50 premium you collected won't make up for the $500 loss on your shares. Covered calls cushion losses, but they don't prevent them. This is why it's important to choose stocks you're comfortable holding even if they dip.

2. You Might Miss a Big Run-Up

Imagine you sell a covered call on XYZ at $20, and then the stock rockets to $30. You'll be forced to sell at $20, missing out on $1,000 in extra profit. That can sting. But here's the mindset: covered calls are about **steady income, not jackpots.** You trade a little upside potential for consistent cash flow.

3. Chasing Premiums (The Rookie Mistake)

When you see an option paying a fat premium, it's tempting to grab it. But bigger premiums often mean bigger risks.

- A premium that looks "too good" usually means the stock is highly volatile.
- Volatile stocks are more likely to crash — or shoot up and take your shares with them.

Stick to stable, boring stocks or ETFs. The goal is consistency. However, I personally have some volatile ones I get in at certain places. As another saying goes, "Higher risk, higher reward."

4. Assignment Risk

If your stock rises above the strike price, your shares will likely get "called away." This isn't always bad (YOU STILL PROFIT), but if you wanted to hold the stock long-term, you'll need to decide whether to buy back in. Some traders get frustrated with assignment but remember: assignment just means you made money.

5. Taxes

In the U.S., premiums from selling covered calls are treated as **short-term capital gains.** That means they're taxed at your ordinary income rate, not the lower long-term capital gains rate.

It's not a dealbreaker, but it's something to plan for — especially if you start generating steady income.

6. Time Commitment

Covered calls aren't a "set it and forget it" strategy. You'll need to check your positions regularly, especially on expiration day. It's not a full-time job, but you can't completely ignore it either.

Putting It All Together

Covered calls are powerful, but they're not magic. The key is understanding what you're trading: **you give up some potential upside in exchange for steady income and a small safety cushion.** The key word being *potential.* If the profit you stand to lose is substantial enough you don't want to have the shares called away, you can always just buy the contract back before expiration. The focus is on the steady income from the premiums. If you spend $1,000 on 10 shares of stock and make back $20 on a premium, that is 2% back. Now if you do that every week, let's say, for just 10 weeks. You have made $200 just selling covered calls on that stock. 20% back on your investment in just 10 weeks!! Yes, it is possible. Or, you can just put your money in the bank earning .01% APY. Where $10,000 will earn you $1 dollar in an entire year. Or just let your money sit in an index fund earning 8-10% average APY. But I am telling you, this strategy works. I do it every week.

If you go in with the right expectations, the risks become manageable, and the strategy becomes a tool you can use for years.

Chapter 7: Weekly Income Plan

The real power of covered calls isn't in a single trade. It's in the habit. Selling one contract here and there is fine, but if you want steady, meaningful income, you need a simple plan you can repeat week after week.

Think of it like a side hustle you run from your phone—one that only takes a few minutes but pays you every week.

Step 1: Choose Your Core Stocks

Pick 1–3 stocks or ETFs you're comfortable holding long-term. These will be your "workhorses."

Good candidates are:

- **Dividend stocks** (income on top of income).
- **Stable ETFs** (less volatile, easier to manage).
- **Boring blue chips** (the slow-and-steady type).

Avoid chasing trendy, high-volatility names unless you're willing to risk the loss on shares, and willing to lose the shares if called away. Consistency beats excitement here.

Step 2: Decide on a Schedule

Most people (like me) choose **weekly expirations** because:

- They generate income faster.
- They give you more flexibility.
- They let you adjust quickly if the market changes.

Monthly options are fine too, especially if you want less screen time. But weekly calls are like getting a paycheck every Friday.

Step 3: Set Your Strike Prices

Each week, pick a strike price slightly above where your stock is trading.

- Example: Stock = $20, Strike = $21.

- This gives you room for profit on the stock if it rises, while still collecting premium.

- If it never hits $21, you keep your stock *and* the cash.

Step 4: Track Your Premiums

Don't just sell calls—record them. Use a simple spreadsheet or notebook to track:

- Date

- Stock

- Strike price

- Expiration date

- Premium collected

- Outcome (expired, assigned, rolled, etc.)

This isn't just bookkeeping. When you look back after 3–6 months and see how much you've made in premiums, it reinforces the power of the strategy. It adds up, and it is motivating to see the weekly income grow.

Step 5: Reinvest or Withdraw

You have two choices with the income you collect:

1. **Reinvest** $\rightarrow$ Use premiums to buy more shares, which eventually lets you sell more covered calls. This compounds your income over time.

2. **Withdraw** $\rightarrow$ Treat it like side income for bills, gas, groceries, or even fun money.

Either choice works—just be intentional. I would not immediately take out the money but perhaps set goals for your weekly income. When you reach that goal, pull half and reinvest half. The more sets of 100 shares you own, the more contracts you can sell, and the more premiums you will collect.

Example: $200/Month Target

Let's say you own 300 shares spread across 3 stocks. Each week, you collect about $15–20 per contract.

- 3 contracts x $15 = $45 per week.

- Over 4 weeks = ~$180.

That's almost $200/month in extra income — just for managing your shares once a week. Scale up your account, and those numbers multiply.

Step 6: Stick With It

The hardest part about covered calls isn't the strategy—it's staying disciplined.

- Don't skip weeks just because premiums look "small." Small adds up.

- Don't chase risky premiums because you feel impatient.

- Don't overthink every trade.

The magic is in the repetition. Week after week, trade after trade, your account becomes a reliable income source.

The Covered Call Mindset

Covered calls won't make you rich overnight. But they *will* pay you consistently—in a way most investments don't.

Think of it like owning a vending machine:

- You don't make $1,000 in a day.
- But you make small, steady profits every week.
- Over time, that adds up to something real.

That's how you should treat covered calls: not as a lottery, but as a reliable side income stream you can build and grow. Something we all need more of is income!

Chapter 8: Scaling Up

Covered calls might start small—$5 here, $20 there—but the real power comes from scaling. As your account grows, the premiums grow too. The system doesn't change, the math just multiplies.

One Contract at a Time

Remember:

- 1 contract = 100 shares.
- The more contracts you can sell, the more premiums you collect.

If one contract pays you $20 per week, then:

- 5 contracts pay you $100 per week.
- 10 contracts pay you $200 per week.
- 25 contracts pay you $500 per week.

Same exact process. Just more shares.

Example: From $50 to $500

Let's say you start small:

- 100 shares of a $10 stock.
- You sell weekly calls and collect $20 each time.
- That's ~$80/month.

Now, over time, you reinvest dividends and premiums to buy more shares. Eventually you build up to 500 shares.

- 500 shares = 5 contracts.
- At $20 per contract, you're now making $100 per week.
- ~$400/month — enough to cover a car payment.

Scale further:

- 1,000 shares = 10 contracts.
- $200 per week = ~$800/month — nearly rent or mortgage territory.

Using Dividends to Scale Faster

Dividend stocks + covered calls are a killer combo. Here's why:

- You get cash from premiums each week.
- You also get dividends every month or quarter.
- If you reinvest both, your share count grows faster.

Eventually, your stock is paying you two ways, and both streams keep multiplying. However, dividend paying stocs do tend to have lower premiums. As their stock prices don't fluctuate much, but there are some good ones. Ford is one. The better the stock, the higher the volume, the higher the premium.

ETFs for Safer Scaling

Owning 1,000 shares of a single company can feel risky. ETFs (like QYLD, SPY, or JEPI) spread your risk across many stocks.

- Premiums may be smaller, but safer.
- Easy to scale since you're not relying on one company's performance.
- More predictable for long-term planning.

Compounding Your Covered Calls

Here's the secret weapon: **don't just spend the income right away.**

If you can, reinvest the premiums to buy more shares. Every extra 100 shares unlocks another contract.

This snowball effect is what turns:

- $20/week → into $200/week → into $2,000/week.

It won't happen overnight. But with discipline, it's achievable in years, not decades.

Realistic Scaling Plan

- Year 1: Start with 100 shares. Learn the ropes.
- Year 2–3: Add more shares through reinvesting. Aim for 500 shares.
- Year 5: With consistent reinvestment, you could realistically reach 1,000+ shares across multiple stocks.
- Long-term: A diversified portfolio of covered call stocks/ETFs, paying you like a second paycheck.

Mindset: From Side Hustle to Income Stream

At first, covered calls might feel like a side hustle—a little extra money. But as you scale, it becomes a genuine income stream that can cover bills, fund vacations, or even supplement retirement.

The system doesn't change. The only thing that changes is your account size and discipline. My first covered call I shared made $5. As of the time of writing this, I made $190 last week. It still isn't much. I am just the average working person like you, trying to get ahead. I scaled up to that in just a few months! I did already have a stock portfolio and moved some stuff around to have 100 shares of a few different stocks. Do the math on that though. $190 a week is $9,880 in a year if I just sell covered calls on what I have and do not reinvest. After taxes, I will still have around $7,500! Imagine doing this for 5, 10, 15 years. I have a goal of reaching $10,000 a month in covered call income, and when (not if) I meet that, I will set another goal for myself. The sky is the limit!

Chapter 9: Bonus Strategy—Cash-Secured Puts

By now, you understand covered calls: you get paid to rent out stocks you already own. But there's another side of the same coin—the **cash-secured put**. This strategy lets you get paid **while** *waiting* **to buy a stock.**

What is a Cash-Secured Put?

When you sell a put option, you're agreeing to buy 100 shares of a stock at a certain price (the *strike price*) if the buyer decides to exercise the option.

To "secure" that promise, you keep enough cash in your account to actually buy those 100 shares. That's why it's called *cash-secured.*

In exchange, the buyer pays you a **premium up front**—money you keep no matter what happens.

How It Works (Plain English)

Imagine you want to buy XYZ stock at $20, but it's currently trading at $22. You'd be happy to own it at $20—just not at today's higher price.

Instead of waiting and hoping it drops, you sell a cash-secured put:

- Strike price: $20
- Expiration: 1 week out
- Premium: $25

Two possible outcomes:

1. **Stock stays above $20** → The option expires worthless. You keep the $25 premium, and you don't have to buy the stock.

2. **Stock drops below $20** → You're assigned, and you buy 100 shares at $20. But remember: you also collected $25, so your *real* cost basis is $19.75.

Either way, you got paid.

Why Use Cash-Secured Puts?

- **Get paid to wait.** Instead of placing a limit order, you earn premium while waiting for your price.

- **Discount on stocks.** If you get assigned, your effective buy price is lower because of the premium collected.

- **Pairs perfectly with covered calls.** Once you're assigned and own the shares, you can immediately start selling covered calls on them. This creates the famous **"wheel strategy."**

Example Trade

- Stock: AGNC at $9.70.

- You want to own it at $9.50.

- You sell a $9.50 put for next week, collecting $15.

Outcomes:

- If AGNC stays above $9.50 → You keep $15. No shares bought.

- If AGNC drops below $9.50 → You buy 100 shares at $9.50, but your real cost is $9.35 (thanks to the $15 premium).

Now you own the stock—and can start selling covered calls on it the following week.

The Wheel Strategy (Optional Advanced Combo)

1. Sell cash-secured puts until you're assigned and buy shares.

2. Sell covered calls on those shares for weekly income.

3. Repeat.

This creates a continuous cycle of premium income, whether you're buying or holding stocks.

Risks to Know

- If the stock crashes far below your strike, you're still obligated to buy at the higher price. (The premium cushions the loss but doesn't eliminate it.)

- Ties up cash: you must keep enough to buy the shares if assigned.

Why I Include This

I added this strategy near the end because it's a natural next step once you're comfortable with covered calls. Many investors combine both strategies to earn income in *any* market—whether stocks are going up, down, or sideways.

Chapter 10: Next Steps

You've made it through the book — from learning what a covered call is, to seeing real examples, to building a weekly income plan. Now it's time to take action.

Covered calls aren't just theory. They're a habit, a process, a system. And like any system, the results come from doing it consistently.

Step 1: Place Your First Trade

Don't wait until you feel like an expert. The best way to learn is by doing. Start small:

- Pick one stock you already own 100 shares of.
- Sell one covered call, even if the premium is just $5 or $10.
- Watch how it plays out.

That first trade will teach you more than a dozen books.

Step 2: Track Your Results

Open a simple spreadsheet or notebook. Record each trade:

- Stock
- Strike price
- Expiration date
- Premium collected
- Outcome (expired, assigned, rolled)

After a month or two, you'll be surprised at how much those small premiums add up.

Step 3: Build a Routine

Consistency is everything. Decide when you'll sell calls each week. Many traders choose Friday afternoons or Monday mornings. Stick to your schedule and treat it like a paycheck.

Step 4: Keep Learning

Covered calls are a foundation. From here, you can explore:

- **Cash-secured puts** (get paid to wait for stocks).
- **The wheel strategy** (combining puts + calls).
- **Dividend growth + covered calls** (double income streams).

You don't have to learn it all at once. Just keep adding to your toolbox.

Step 5: Manage Expectations

Remember:

- Covered calls won't make you a millionaire overnight.
- The goal is **steady, repeatable income.**
- $20 here, $50 there, $200 a month—it adds up over time.

If you stay disciplined, that side income grows into something powerful.

Step 6: Join a Community

Trading can feel lonely. Find other people learning covered calls. Join forums, follow newsletters, connect with groups. When you share ideas and experiences, you grow faster.

Step 7: Take the Long View

Covered calls are a lifelong skill. Imagine:

- A retirement account that pays you income every month.

- A stock portfolio that acts like a second job.

- The confidence of knowing your money is working, even when you're not.

That's the vision. That's the next step.

Final Words

Covered calls are about freedom. Not the kind of freedom that comes from hitting a jackpot, but the kind that comes from small, steady wins—wins that stack up over time.

Your journey doesn't end here. It starts with your first covered call, your first premium, your first "aha" moment. And from there, the only limit is how far you want to take it.

So open your brokerage app. Look at your stocks. And take the next step.

Glossary

Assignment – When the buyer of your option decides to exercise it. If you sold a covered call, this means your shares are "called away" at the strike price.

Brokerage – The financial platform you use to buy and sell stocks and options (examples: Robinhood, Fidelity, Webull).

Cash-Secured Put – An options strategy where you sell a put contract while keeping enough cash set aside to buy 100 shares if assigned. It's a way to get paid while waiting to buy stock.

Contract – A standardized agreement to buy or sell 100 shares of a stock at a set price (the strike price) before a set date (the expiration).

Covered Call – An options strategy where you sell a call option against shares you already own. You collect a premium up front and agree to sell your stock at the strike price if assigned.

Dividend – A cash payment some companies give to shareholders, usually monthly or quarterly. Dividends can be combined with covered calls for double income.

Expiration Date – The last day an option contract is valid. After this date, the contract either expires worthless or is exercised/assigned.

Gains (Capital Gains) – Profit you make when the value of a stock goes up. If you sell at a higher price than you bought, the difference is your gain.

Income (Premium Income) – The cash you collect when you sell an option. With covered calls, the premium is yours to keep whether or not the stock is called away.

In the Money (ITM) – When an option has value if exercised. For a call option, that means the stock price is above the strike price.

Limit Order – An order to buy or sell at a specific price or better. Often used when selling options to make sure you receive a minimum premium.

Option – A financial contract that gives the buyer the right (but not the obligation) to buy or sell 100 shares of stock at a set price before a set date.

Options Chain – The list of all available option contracts for a stock, showing strike prices, expiration dates, and premiums.

Out of the Money (OTM) – When an option has no value if exercised. For a call option, that means the stock price is below the strike price.

Premium – The price paid by the buyer of an option. As the seller of a covered call, you collect this amount up front as income.

Rolling – Closing one option trade and immediately opening another with a later expiration date or different strike price. Used to adjust or extend covered calls.

Strike Price – The price at which an option buyer can purchase (calls) or sell (puts) the stock. For covered calls, this is the price you agree to sell your shares if assigned.

Volatility – How much a stock's price moves up and down. Higher volatility usually means higher option premiums, but also higher risk. It means the stock has lower "valleys" and higher "peaks"

Wheel Strategy – A cycle where you sell cash-secured puts until assigned, then sell covered calls on the shares you now own, repeating the process for continuous income.

About the Author

Adrian Gregory is an entrepreneur, writer, and self-taught investor with a passion for making finance simple for everyday people. After years of studying the markets on his own, Adrian discovered the power of covered calls — a strategy that creates steady income from stocks without the need for risky speculation.

He believes that anyone, no matter their background or account size, can learn to make their money work harder with straightforward strategies explained in plain English.

When he isn't trading or writing, Adrian runs a braille transcription business dedicated to accessibility, designs puzzles and books, and spends time with his wife and daughters in Tennessee.

You can connect with Adrian and follow his ongoing insights at his Substack newsletter: **Adrian / @adrian716731**

Appendix: Stocks & ETFs to Watch

At the time of writing this:

1. High Dividend Yield Stocks

These stocks and REITs stand out for their income potential, many with dividend yields above 5%—appealing if you're looking to layer dividends with premium income. As of recent data:

- **Two Harbors Investment Corp (TWO)** — ~16% yield
- **Lument Finance Trust (LFT)** — ~12% yield
- **Sunrise Realty Trust (SUNS)** — ~11% yield
- **AG Mortgage Investment Trust (MITT)** — ~11% yield
- **Bristol Myers Squibb (BMY)** — ~5.4% yield
- **Edison International (EIX)** — ~6% yield
- **Prudential Financial (PRU)** — ~5.2% yield
- **Interpublic Group (IPG)** — ~5.3% yield
- **Realty Income (O)** — monthly-paying REIT, famed for steady dividends
- **Dividend Aristocrats (S&P 500 companies with 25+ years of dividend increases)** such as **PepsiCo (PEP)**, **Johnson & Johnson (JNJ)**, **ExxonMobil (XOM)**, and many others

2. Stocks with Heavy Options Activity

When you're using strategies like covered calls, liquidity and tight spreads matter. These are symbols where options are highly active, making execution smoother:

- **Tesla (TSLA)** — averaging ~700,000 daily contracts

- **Apple (AAPL)**

- **Nvidia (NVDA)**

- **Amazon (AMZN)**

- **AMD, Meta (META), Microsoft (MSFT), AMC, Google (GOOGL/GOOG)**

3. High-Yield Option-Income ETFs

These ETFs use options strategies (like covered calls or option income overlays) to deliver elevated yields:

- A range of **YieldMax Option-Income ETFs**, with yields potentially exceeding 50–70% (yes, that's real—though high yields often come with higher risk)

- Examples include: **YieldMax Universe Fund (YMAX)**, **YieldMax AMD Option Income Strategy ETF (AMDY)**, **YieldMax Tesla (TSLY)**, **YieldMax NVDA (NVDY)**, and several others

How to Use This List

- **Covered Calls Setup**: Start with high-dividend or stable stocks like Realty Income (O), WPC, or Dividend Aristocrats for a conservative income strategy.

- **Liquidity Focus**: If you want tight executions, consider TSLA, AAPL, NVDA, or AMZN—for regular covered-call activity or rolling.

- **Passive Option Income**: For a hands-off approach, consider YieldMax ETFs which come pre-packaged with options income strategies.

(Friendly reminder: Always do your own research before buying. High yields often come with higher risks. This is not financial advice. I am not a financial advisor. I only try to educate the everyday investor.)

Appendix B: 5 Rookie Mistakes to Avoid with Covered Calls

Covered calls are simple — but like anything in investing, the little details matter. Beginners often trip over the same handful of mistakes. Avoid these, and you'll already be ahead of most traders.

Mistake 1: Chasing the Biggest Premiums

It's tempting to scroll through the options chain and grab the fattest premium you can find. But big premiums almost always come with big risk.

Why? Because they usually belong to volatile stocks. High volatility = bigger chance of the stock swinging wildly, getting called away, or dropping hard.

The Fix: Stick to steady, boring stocks or ETFs. Aim for consistency, not lottery tickets. Covered calls are about collecting rent, not winning jackpots.

Mistake 2: Selling Too Close to the Money

Selling calls right at (or even below) the current stock price gives you the most premium — but it almost guarantees your shares will get called away if the stock moves even slightly up.

The Fix: Give yourself breathing room. Choose a strike price a little above where the stock is trading. That way, you still collect premium and you leave space for the stock to rise before you risk assignment.

Mistake 3: Forgetting About Earnings and News

Earnings announcements, product launches, or big news events can cause stocks to jump or crash overnight. If you sell a call right before earnings, don't be surprised if your stock soars past your strike price and your shares get called away.

👉 The Fix: Check the calendar before placing trades. Avoid selling calls right before earnings or other major news. Or, if you do, accept the risk of losing your shares.

Mistake 4: Ignoring Taxes

Premiums from covered calls are considered **short-term capital gains** in the U.S. That means they're taxed at your ordinary income rate. If you start generating steady income, the tax bill can sneak up on you.

👉 The Fix: Keep track of your premiums. Set aside a portion for taxes, or do your trading inside a tax-advantaged account like an IRA (where allowed).

Mistake 5: Overcomplicating Things

Beginners sometimes try to mix covered calls with every advanced options strategy they find online. They roll too often, jump between stocks, or chase setups they don't fully understand.

👉 The Fix: Keep it simple. Start with one or two reliable stocks. Sell one covered call per week or month. Get comfortable with the basics before layering on complexity.

Final Word

Everyone makes mistakes at first. The key is learning from them and not repeating them. Covered calls are most powerful when you keep it **steady, boring, and repeatable.**

Avoid these rookie errors, and you'll already be ahead of most people trying to trade options.

Appendix C: Brokerages with Options Trading

Before you can sell your first covered call, you'll need a brokerage account that supports options trading. Not all brokers are equal — some are beginner-friendly, while others are built for more advanced traders. Below is a list of popular choices (U.S.-based) along with their strengths.

Robinhood

- **Best for**: Absolute beginners.

- **Pros**: Clean, simple interface; commission-free trades; easy to sell covered calls right from the app.

- **Cons**: Limited research tools; not as advanced as other platforms.

Webull

- **Best for**: Beginners who want more data.

- **Pros**: Free trading; good charting tools; supports extended-hours trading.

- **Cons**: Slightly more complex interface; can overwhelm first-timers.

Fidelity

- **Best for**: Long-term investors who also want to sell options.
- **Pros**: Great customer service; strong research; no commissions; excellent for retirement accounts.
- **Cons**: Options interface isn't as sleek as Robinhood or Webull.

Charles Schwab

- **Best for**: All-around investors.
- **Pros**: Wide range of investment choices; strong research and support; great for building long-term wealth *and* trading.
- **Cons**: More features than most beginners need.

TD Ameritrade (Thinkorswim Platform)

- **Best for**: Traders who want advanced tools.
- **Pros**: Professional-grade software; paper trading to practice; tons of data.
- **Cons**: Steep learning curve; may feel intimidating at first.

E*TRADE

- **Best for**: Investors who want balance.
- **Pros**: User-friendly website/app; good options education; no commissions.
- **Cons**: Not as slick as Robinhood/Webull; fewer advanced features than TD Ameritrade.

Interactive Brokers (IBKR)

- **Best for**: Experienced traders and global investing.

- **Pros**: Access to global markets; very low fees for high-volume traders; advanced options strategies supported.
- **Cons**: Overwhelming for beginners; best if you want to go beyond simple covered calls.

SoFi Invest

- **Best for**: Beginners who also want financial tools.
- **Pros**: Easy-to-use app; integrates with personal finance/loan products; commission-free.
- **Cons**: Fewer advanced options tools compared to bigger brokers.

Choosing the Right Broker

- **If you're brand new**: Robinhood or Webull keep it simple.
- **If you want retirement + trading**: Fidelity or Schwab.
- **If you want pro-level features**: TD Ameritrade or Interactive Brokers.

Ultimately, the "best" broker is the one you'll actually use comfortably every week.

This book also available in E-Book format on Amazon. Please leave a review if you like it on Amazon and PayHip website. Scan the QR Code Below to explore more books, resources, and free tools at:

https://payhip.com/SecondSightPublishing

Etsy Store:

https://secondsighthub.etsy.com

www.ingramcontent.com/pod-product-compliance
Lightning Source LLC
Chambersburg PA
CBHW071518210326
41597CB00018B/2811